MICHAEL R. SEATON
with Jared Yaple

BECOMING A GOOD SAMARITAN

TEEN EDITION // SIX SESSIONS

ZONDERVAN®   World Vision
Building a better world for children

ZONDERVAN.com/
AUTHORTRACKER
follow your favorite authors

ZONDERVAN

Becoming a Good Samaritan Teen Edition Participant's Guide
Copyright © 2012 by Michael R. Seaton

Requests for information should be addressed to:
Zondervan, *Grand Rapids, Michigan 49530*

ISBN 978-0-310-89259-5

Published in association with the literary agency of Alive Communications, Inc., 7680 Goddard Street, Suite 200, Colorado Springs, CO 80920. www.alivecommunications.com

Cover design: Gearbox
Cover photography: Tomas Bercic/Getty Images; Masterfile; David Uttley/Luminescent Images
Interior design: Ben Fetterley

Printed in the United States of America

12 13 14 15 16 17 /DCI/ 23 22 21 20 19 18 17 16 15 14 13 12 11 10 9 8 7 6 5 4 3 2 1

Contents

Change Begins Here

Zach Hunter

We have to start with ourselves. We must undergo a change in our thinking, finding a deeper commitment to helping "others," and maybe even a new sense of wonder about what could be and how we can be a part of making that "could be" happen. Ultimately, the change needs to happen within our hearts. For those of us who call ourselves Christians, that means seeking God diligently and yielding ourselves to him, asking him to change us and give us a new set of priorities and a deeper love for all people.

If we're really going to follow Jesus, we need to make sure our priorities are in line with his priorities. Over the past few years I've been amazed at the amount of teaching in the Bible that focuses on how we are supposed to treat the poor. I had no idea what a huge priority this was to God.

People sometimes say that those of us who claim to follow Jesus are self-centered and focused on our own comforts and wishes. They think Christians seem petty and small-minded. It bothers me that this might be how some people view me and my friends who follow Jesus — especially since that's so far from what God calls us to be. I was reading in the ancient book of Isaiah and discovered an interesting section where God talks about his priorities:

> *Is not this the kind of fasting I have chosen:*
> *to loose the chains of injustice*
> *and untie the cords of the yoke,*
> *to set the oppressed free*
> *and break every yoke?*
> *Is it not to share your food with the hungry*
> *and to provide the poor wanderer with shelter —*
> *when you see the naked, to clothe [them],*

and not to turn away from your own flesh and blood?
Then your light will break forth like the dawn,
and your healing will quickly appear;
then your righteousness will go before you,
and the glory of the LORD will be your rear guard.
Then you will call, and the LORD will answer;
you will cry for help, and he will say: Here am I.
If you do away with the yoke of oppression,
with the pointing finger and malicious talk,
and if you spend yourselves in behalf of the hungry
and satisfy the needs of the oppressed,
then your light will rise in the darkness,
and your night will become like the noonday.

That's from the 58th chapter of Isaiah (vv. 6 – 10). It's pretty radical. God says that if we spend ourselves on behalf of the hungry, and if we focus our attention on taking care of the poor, the hurting, and the oppressed, then we will shine. I think people who shine and reflect the goodness of God might be an answer to the criticisms many make about Christians.

Paraphrased from Zach Hunter, *Generation Change* (Zondervan, 2011)

How to Use This Guide

Thank you for choosing to **start>**! This guide is designed to accompany the *start> Becoming a Good Samaritan Teen Edition* DVD. Our hope is that you will rally a few of your friends to meet at church, or simply around a table at your local coffee shop, and work through each of the six sessions in turn. The sessions are brief—each takes about an hour—and can be completed at the speed you decide—weekly, every other week, monthly, or whatever works for you.

You'll notice that each session contains two major sections: "Group Time" and "Personal Time." Plan to complete the entire "Group Time" portion with your group. Use the time designations noted beside each session subheading to do so. Then, work through the "Personal Time" section between group meetings on your own. Here's how the Group Time breaks out:

- **Get Connected** (1 minute)—read a brief overview of the session content
- **Know Your Neighbor** (2 minutes)—share your current beliefs or understandings about the topic
- **Give Your Heart and Mind to God** (1 minute)—ask for God's guidance as you begin the session
- **Learn Together** (20 minutes)—watch the session video on the DVD
- **Discussion** (30 minutes)—talk about ideas and insights sparked by the DVD session
- **Now Is the Time** (5 minutes)—it's your turn to put your faith in action
- **Close with Prayer** (1 minute)—finish your group time with prayer

Ready to **start>**? All you need is a few friends, a TV or computer with DVD capability, a Bible, a pen or pencil, and this guide. To connect with others who are becoming Good Samaritans, visit www.startproject .org. There you'll find information and opportunities that will encourage, educate, and inspire you to **start>**. The Good Samaritan journey is the path God intends for *all* of his followers to walk. We're excited that you've decided to take the first step.

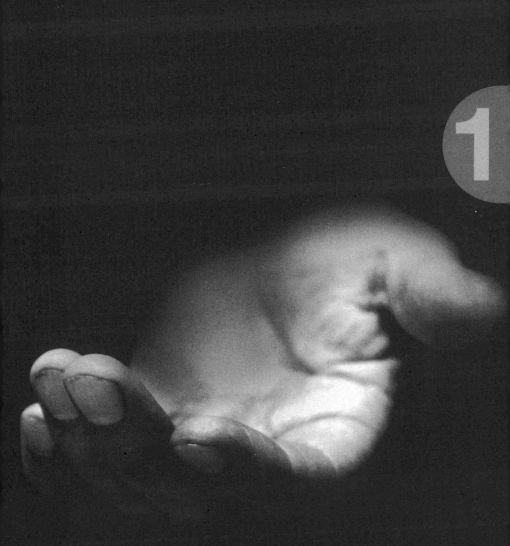

1

Becoming a Good Samaritan

> "I am only one, but I am one. I cannot do everything, but I can do something."
>
> — Edward Everett Hale, 19th century U. S. author

 start> Group Time

 Get Connected   1 minute

Have someone in the group read aloud this brief description of the session theme.

An article in the January/February 2009 issue of *Good* magazine attempted to sum up the state of planet Earth. What was not necessarily inspiring in the article were details about the challenges the Earth presently faces: a bad economy, ongoing war, threats of disease and hunger and poverty. But what did carry hope was the conclusion the author drew:

> *The global problems are larger than before ... but our capacity to meet them is larger still.*

The truth is that followers of Jesus — people like you — are capable of doing what no other people can do: unite together with love and passion to help bring healing and reconciliation to every heart, soul, and corner of the world.

In this opening session you are invited to explore what it means to move from *what you believe* to *how those beliefs get acted out* on behalf of those in need around you. If every man, woman, student, and child who call themselves followers of Jesus Christ will join the fight against today's biggest threats, the world will change.

Your actions matter. Your choices matter. Choose today to **start>**.

> Know Your Neighbor   2 minutes

Using one or two words, answer the following question about the session theme.

Why aren't there more "Good Samaritans" in the world today?

"In everything I did, I showed you that by this kind of hard work we must help the weak, remembering the words the Lord Jesus himself said: 'It is more blessed to give than to receive.'"

— Acts 20:35

> Give Your Heart and Mind to God   1 minute

Before the Good Samaritan in Luke 10 could *act* well, he first had to *see* well. As you prepare your heart and mind for session 1, open in prayer, asking God for eyes to *really* see the people in need where you live. Who are they? What is life like for them? What spiritual needs do they have, in addition to their physical needs? What resources do you already possess that could help meet a need today? Thank God for giving you eyes that can see, hands that can serve, and a heart that can beat fast for the things that bring him joy.

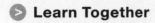 **Learn Together** 20 minutes

If you'd like to take notes as you watch the session 1 video segment, use the space below.

> **Discuss "Becoming a Good Samaritan"**   30 minutes

1. As you listened to the parable of the Good Samaritan, what words, phrases, or ideas struck you?

2. In *The Message* paraphrase of the Bible, Luke 10:27 reads this way: "Love the Lord your God with all your passion and prayer and muscle and intelligence — and ... love your neighbor as well as you do yourself." When have you seen followers of Jesus you know "loving the Lord their God" with *each* of the following aspects of their lives? For example, maybe you have a friend who loves to pray for others, or you have a teacher who sings in the worship team at church.

   Passion

   Prayer

cont.

Muscle/Strength

Intelligence

3. Through which of the four aspects do you most often sense the love of God flowing out of your own life? Which of the four seems to be the most challenging for you? Share life experiences you've had that help explain your responses.

4. In your view, why is it so important for followers of Jesus to show love in all four ways? Discuss your thoughts with the group.

5. Real joy is found in real obedience to the commands of Jesus. As Miles McPherson said, "You can't enter into the joy of the Lord unless you're faithful to do the things that he said to do." If Jesus desires that you faithfully do the things he said to do, then he will equip you to do them. What assurances from God might help you to overcome the fears and obstacles that you face? Write your thoughts in the space below, sharing one or two of them with your group.

> Now Is the Time   5 minutes

This is the most important part of the session — when you decide how you and your group will choose to live like the Good Samaritan.

In the spirit of getting your hands dirty today, brainstorm with your group five to seven acts of service that would reflect your love for God in a "physical and present" way. Write down your thoughts on the lines below and on the next page; then choose one that you will accomplish as a group between now and when you meet again. An example has been provided to help get you started.

Service Ideas

Ex. Donate food to local food bank

- _____
- _____
- _____

- _____
- _____
- _____
- _____

❯ Close with Prayer   1 minute

The end of your time together is now the beginning of incredible Good Samaritan opportunities for you and your group. Take a moment to say a prayer to God, saying thank you for what you have learned and committing your life to living like the Good Samaritan.

start> Personal Time

Living out your faith in real and tangible ways is more than just doing a DVD study — it is a lifelong journey. The "Personal Time" section is your guide as you go forward on this quest. Of course, like any journey, this one will be easier and more fruitful with the support and encouragement of others. **startproject.org** *is that community. There you'll find other stories and testimonies just like yours, links to organizations and people who need your help and special skills, and opportunities to Learn, Live, and Lead a Good Samaritan life.*

To reconnect with this session's topic as you dive into the "start> Now" section, answer the following questions.

1. John Ortberg said that "the adventure of compassion is the journey for which you were made." What does the phrase "adventure of compassion" mean to you? Do you believe you're part of that adventure today?

2. Jim Wallis stated, "Things change when a new generation decides, 'this that was acceptable is no longer tolerable,' or, 'that which we thought impossible, now we believe can be done.'" Do you feel that your generation is capable of doing things for God that seem impossible? Write three things below that you believe must be *no longer tolerable* in this world, things that with God's power and presence you hope to see overcome.

- _____
- _____
- _____

> start> NOW

*Everyone must **start>** at the beginning, which means going from little or no knowledge to enough understanding to be able to make wise decisions. In each session, this portion of the Personal Time will provide you with resources and links to a wealth of important information.*

LEARN

● **Soak in Scripture.** Open your Bible and read Isaiah 6:8. Ask God what he would have you do to become more "sendable" today.

● **Inspire generosity.** Visit Lynne Hybels' website and read her article titled, "A Call for Unprecedented Generosity" (www.lynnehybels.com). Make a list of ways that you and your friends could "spend less on your wants so that [you] can give more to others' needs."

● **Take stock.** Keep track of every hour that you spend today. Before going to bed, review your choices and ask yourself if your life is being spent in ways that honor God and those in need around you.

● **Pray dangerously.** Pray like Isaiah, telling God that you are ready to "be sent" to a broken and needy world.

LIVE

● **Talk it up.** Memorize and share Amos 5:24 with a friend or family member today. Discuss what you both believe the verse is saying.

● **Go on a need hunt.** Stop by your local shelter, fire station, nursing home, or hospital and ask what current needs exist. Resolve to meet one simple need you uncover.

● **Invite a friend.** Ask a friend to join you at your next **start>** meeting. It's not too late to involve others in the quest to become Good Samaritans!

● **Give it away.** Give away a material possession to someone who needs it more than you do. Write in a journal about how it felt to put into practice the words of Acts 20:35, which says, "It is more blessed to give than to receive."

LEAD

● **Pray to have impact; pray to be impacted.** Pray for the people whom you will meet and serve throughout this **start>** experience. Ask God not only how you might impact their lives, but also what you might learn from *them*. Lead your group in prayer along these lines the next time you meet.

● **Lead your leaders.** Encourage your church leaders to make *start>*

Becoming a Good Samaritan available to the entire congregation if they haven't already done so.

● **Surf the Web.** Rally two or three friends to join you online at www .startproject.org. Review the material there, start a new group or discussion, and pray for God to bless each one of them for their selfless contribution to **start>**.

Former World Vision International President Dean Hirsch says that whenever he has chosen to reach out and serve someone in need, even in a seemingly insignificant way, he remembers the words of Mother Teresa: "Remember, God did not call you to be successful; he called you to be faithful."

> Read

- *Generation Change*, Zach Hunter
- *Do Hard Things*, Alex and Brett Harris
- *Passion to Action*, Jay and Beth Loecken
- *It's Not about Me*, Max Lucado
- *Leave a Footprint*, Tim Baker

> Watch

- *Pay It Forward* (PG-13)
- *To Save a Life* (PG-13)
- *New* (NR)

> Surf

- www.startproject.org
- www.worldvision.org
- www.seekjustice.org
- www.one.org
- www.passiontoaction.org

Caring for the Sick

2

> "Let no one ever come to you without leaving better."
>
> — Mother Teresa

 start> Group Time

 Get Connected   1 minute

Have someone in the group read aloud this brief description of the session theme.

General Colin Powell once said, "No war on the face of the earth is more destructive than the AIDS pandemic." And with the current stats on HIV/AIDS — the first epidemic of a new disease since the fifteenth century — you'd think Powell would be correct. According to the 2008 *UN AIDS Report on the Global AIDS Epidemic,* AIDS now has spread to every country in the world; every day, nearly 7,400 people become infected with HIV and more than 5,400 people die from AIDS; and the estimated number of deaths per year are nearly two million people.

But for all of the carnage caused by AIDS, it is hardly in a category alone. In fact, based on current United Nations findings, more children die today of malaria than of AIDS — a sobering reality, given that malaria is a preventable disease.

During this session you will be invited to take a closer look at the impact of pandemics such as AIDS and malaria in both the U.S. and in countries abroad, and answer the question, "What role does a follower of Jesus have in preventing and treating these fatal diseases?"

Your actions matter. Your choices matter. Choose today to **start>**.

> Know Your Neighbor   2 minutes

Using one or two words, answer the following question about the session theme.

In Jesus' day, lepers were not to be touched. Who are the "untouchables" of today's society?

"He heals the brokenhearted and binds up their wounds."

—Psalm 147:3

> Give Your Heart and Mind to God   1 minute

Followers of Jesus understand that they were once "untouchable" because of their sin. But it was in the midst of that untouchable state that the God of heaven and earth wrapped himself in human flesh in the person of Jesus and came to touch the world with freedom and healing and grace. For those who have been freed, it's time to free others. For those who have been healed, it's time to heal others. For those who have tasted grace, it's time to give that gift to those who crave to be touched.

As you begin session 2, ask God to remind you of what it was like to be stuck in your sickness — and then to be the recipient of a healing hand to help you up. Invite him to stir you and move you and prompt you to action on behalf of someone who is sick today — whether spiritually, emotionally, financially, or physically. Ask God how you might be his conduit of grace and healing today.

> **Learn Together**   20 minutes

If you'd like to take notes as you watch the session 2 video segment, use the space below.

> Discuss "Caring for the Sick" 30 minutes

1. Think about the last time you were sick. Did you have the necessary resources to find a remedy and recuperate, including things like easy access to health care, inexpensive medications, the support of friends and family, and so forth? On the grid below, list the resources you had at your disposal that helped you get back your health. Then note the implications of having access to each resource and discuss your observations with the group. An example has been provided to get you started.

Resource I Relied On	Impact of Having Access to This Resource
Ex. Ability to be sick and still go to school	*Was able to stay caught up on schoolwork*

2. For many people, poverty and disease go hand-in-hand. Take a look at the following four choices that are made week in and week out by thousands of people living on less than a dollar a day.

Purchase malaria medication	**or**	Use that money to send children to school
Buy one can of clean water	**or**	Buy food for a week's worth of once-a-day meals
Spend money on a bed net	**or**	Hold the money back for a bag of grain
Inoculate a newborn daughter	**or**	Save the money to visit dying father two countries away

Now imagine what life would be like if you had to make no-win decisions such as these on a daily or weekly basis. What are some of the spiritual, financial, emotional, physical, and relational consequences you might face? Discuss your thoughts with your group.

> Now Is the Time   5 minutes

This is the most important part of the session — deciding how you and your group will choose to live like the Good Samaritan.

In the video session Jeanne Stevens said that while you may only be one person — you are one and you can begin by just doing one thing, and that each action is "a step forward instead of just standing still." We can notice. We can see. We can talk. We can pray. We can help. See the sign. Hear God. *Please* touch. Think of someone you know who is sick in his or her body or who has been cast aside by "better functioning" members of society. Maybe it's a personal friend, or perhaps it is someone who suffers half a world away.

> How might God be asking you to reach out to that person with a loving touch from him? Write that person's name on the line below and then respond to the four starter ideas below it.
>
> God, help me to touch: _____
>
> The needs that I see in his/her life:
>
>
>
> What I can say:
>
>
>
> What I can pray:
>
>
>
> How I can help:

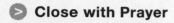

> Close with Prayer   1 minute

The end of your time together is now the beginning of incredible Good Samaritan possibilities for you and your group. Take a moment to say a prayer to God, saying thank you for what you have learned and committing your life to living like the Good Samaritan.

start> Personal Time

Living out your faith in real and tangible ways is more than just doing a DVD study—it is a lifelong journey. The "Personal Time" section is your guide as you go forward on this quest. Of course, like any journey, this one will be easier and more fruitful with the support and encouragement of others. **startproject.org** *is that community. There you'll find other stories and testimonies just like yours, links to organizations and people who need your help and special skills, and opportunities to Learn, Live, and Lead a Good Samaritan life.*

To reconnect with this session's topic as you dive into the "start> Now" section, answer the following questions.

1. Session teacher Kay Warren said that after her first trip to Africa, she found herself judging not other people, but herself. "I had to ask, what would I do? What *was* I doing?" Kay said. "And the answer was, *nothing*." When have you ever found yourself in a similar situation, feeling fearful and overwhelmed as you consider the AIDS pandemic? Note the fears or emotions you felt in the space below.

2. Global AIDS expert Christo Greyling said that upon manifesting his first AIDS symptoms, he knew that time was running out. Greyling told his wife, "I want to be a witness for Christ, using this situation of HIV while I'm still healthy enough to do it." As you consider your life, what are you "healthy enough to do" today in terms of helping eradicate preventable disease?

 start> NOW

Everyone must **start>** *at the beginning, which means going from little or no knowledge to enough understanding to be able to make wise decisions. In each session, this portion of the Personal Time will provide you with resources and links to a wealth of important information.*

LEARN

● **Give thanks for good health.** Respond to Dr. Thomas Fuller's 18th century quote, "Health is not valued until sickness comes." What thoughts, values, or beliefs do his words stir up in your spirit?

● **Visit your own backyard.** Is there someone in your community who is actively involved in meeting the needs of people suffering with preventable and treatable diseases? Invite them to participate in your **start>** discussions to glean insights and learn of user-friendly ways you and your group might participate locally.

● **Watch your water.** The EPA estimates that more than 80 percent of infant mortality in the undeveloped world happens because of unsafe drinking water. Assuming you have access to clean drinking water, as a way to get in touch with just how fortunate you are, log your water intake for one full day. Each time you brush your teeth, take a shower, or down a quick 8 ounces of cool refreshment, offer a prayer of thanksgiving to God.

LIVE

● **Lend your voice.** Lend your voice to people suffering with HIV and AIDS by joining the ONE Campaign today. Visit www.one.org for details.

● **Take an "H₂0 Challenge."** Assuming you have no health restrictions, for two weeks drink nothing but water and donate the money you would normally spend on soda, coffee, smoothies, and other beverages to World Vision or another organization that drills clean-water wells in developing countries. Keep a journal during your experience.

● **Give care.** Have your group assemble a Caregiver Kit that equips a trained World Vision frontline caregiver with essential supplies such as soap, washcloths, and latex gloves that can improve and prolong the lives of those living with AIDS, as well as help prevent the spread of the disease. For more information, go to www. worldvision.org.

● **Love a child.** Sponsor a HopeChild through World Vision and help turn the tide on AIDS by responding to the specific needs of children in communities affected by the disease. For more information, go to www.worldvision.org.

LEAD

● **Invite God's interventions.** Start a weekly or monthly prayer group that meets to understand and pray for global health issues. Consider highlighting one people group, country, or disease each time you convene, and then invite participants to serve in ways that stretch them emotionally, spiritually, and financially between sessions.

● **Host a guest speaker.** Invite a guest speaker to your school, youth group, or **start>** group to help educate your community on effective ways to serve sufferers of pandemics worldwide.

● **Get cooking!** Coordinate an event, such as a breakfast gathering or dinner fundraiser, to raise awareness and energize people about getting involved in the fight against preventable or treatable diseases. Be sure to provide suggestions for straightforward ways that people can make a quick-hitting, tangible difference in their corner of the world.

> Read

- *Where Is God When It Hurts?* Philip Yancey
- *When God Weeps*, Joni Eareckson Tada
- *Mountains Beyond Mountains*, Tracy Kidder
- *Dangerous Surrender*, Kay Warren
- *Warrior Princess*, Princess Kasune Zulu

> Watch

- *My Sister's Keeper* (PG-13)
- *A Walk to Remember* (PG)
- *Letters to God* (PG)

> Surf

- www.startproject.org
- www.endmalaria.org
- www.doctorswithoutborders.org
- www.charitywater.org
- www.one.org

Seeking Justice

3

> "God has a plan to help bring justice to the world — and his plan is us!"
>
> — Gary Haugen, founder of International Justice Mission

  Group Time

> **Get Connected** 1 minute

Have someone in the group read aloud this brief description of the session theme.

All people are "God's kind" of people — people who were created in the image of Almighty God and for an intentional purpose. And while most followers of Jesus agree that all people should be treated with dignity and respect, sadly this is not always the case.

What is the role of followers of Jesus in reconciling broken and bruised relationships in today's world? It is, according to the well-known words of Micah 6:8, "to act justly, and to love mercy [kindness], and to walk humbly with your God." Those are interesting words to consider because they imply that kindness and humility alone are not enough. It is the seeking out of *justice*, as well, that will prove to a watching world that the God we serve is good.

Your actions matter. Your choices matter. Choose today to **start>**.

> Know Your Neighbor

Using one or two words, answer the following question about the session theme.

Where does "injustice" exist in today's world?

"To do what is right and just is more acceptable to the LORD than sacrifice."

— Proverbs 21:3

> Give Your Heart and Mind to God

In Isaiah 1:17, the prophet gave instruction on God's behalf according to a vision he had regarding Judah and Jerusalem. "Learn to do right," said Isaiah, "seek justice. Defend the oppressed. Take up the cause of the fatherless; plead the case of the widow."

It's clear that God has high expectations for involvement in getting rid of injustices in the world in which we live, but equally important is God's expectation for what we do *before* we seek justice. In the verse that precedes Isaiah's list of commands, he tells the people — and followers of Jesus today — "Wash and make yourselves clean. Take your evil deeds out of my sight; stop doing wrong."

As you enter session 3, ask God to show you areas in your life that need to be washed clean by his power, so that you will be able to approach the task of justice-seeking with pure hands and a spotless heart.

> Learn Together   20 minutes

If you'd like to take notes as you watch the session 3 video segment, use the space below.

> Discuss "Seeking Justice" 30 minutes

1. Gary Haugen, founder of International Justice Mission, defined injustice as taking from people what's inherently theirs. Among your group, what "common inheritances" do you enjoy? Note your answers below, and then discuss your insights.

2. "God wants us to do his work of justice in the world," said Haugen, "but he invites us to be his plan — his instruments — for doing it." Who comes to mind when you think of someone who has invested his or her life to make sure other people could realize their common inheritance? What did his or her involvement look like?

Now Is the Time

This is the most important part of the session — deciding how you and your group will choose to live like the Good Samaritan.

In the video segment you were introduced to the first recorded sermon of Jesus, found in Luke 4:

> *The Spirit of the Lord is on me, because he has anointed me to proclaim the good news to the poor. He has sent me to proclaim freedom for the prisoners and recovery of sight for the blind, to set the oppressed free, to proclaim the year of the Lord's favor. (vv. 18 – 19)*

This passage makes it clear that when it comes to the teachings of Jesus, it all starts with justice and mercy and compassion. In the words of Jarrett Stevens, Jesus "invites ordinary everyday people like you and me to join him, whether it's around the world or around the corner" on a journey of justice and compassion.

In response, what sermon is God asking you to give with your words and life?

How can you join Jesus on a journey of justice and compassion in your school? Your neighborhood? The world?

How will you **start>** today?

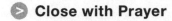

> Close with Prayer
1 minute

The end of your time together is now the beginning of incredible Good Samaritan possibilities for you and your group. Take a moment to say a prayer to God, saying thank you for what you have learned and committing your life to living like the Good Samaritan.

*Living out your faith in real and tangible ways is more than just doing a DVD study — it is a lifelong journey. The "Personal Time" section is your guide as you go forward on this quest. Of course, like any journey, this one will be easier and more fruitful with the support and encouragement of others. **startproject.org** is that community. There you'll find other stories and testimonies just like yours, links to organizations and people who need your help and special skills, and opportunities to Learn, Live, and Lead a Good Samaritan life.*

To reconnect with this session's topic as you dive into the "start> Now" section, answer the questions below.

1. Gary Haugen said that two of the more unfamiliar passions of God are his passion for *the world* and his passion for *justice*. If your close friends and family were polled, how well would they say your life reflects those two passions? Are you satisfied with what you think they would say? Why or why not?

2. Teen activist Zach Hunter began his work toward abolishing slavery before he was a teenager. "There's a place at the table of activism even for a twelve-year-old!" he said. Hunter didn't

allow his youthfulness to keep film from getting in the game. What are a few of the perceived obstacles you see in your life that threaten to keep you sidelined from making a difference in the area of justice? Note them in the space —below; then ask God to help replace your fears and assumptions with confidence and strength.

> start> NOW

*Everyone must **start>** at the beginning, which means going from little or no knowledge to enough understanding to be able to make wise decisions. In each session, this portion of the Personal Time will provide you with resources and links to a wealth of important information.*

LEARN

● **Get in the loop.** Visit the International Justice Mission website (www.ijm .org) to learn more about how you can help fight human trafficking worldwide.

● **Shop responsibly.** Trade as One (www.tradeasone.org) provides an opportunity for you to change lives with everything you buy. Whether it's a unique gift or an everyday product like chocolate, your spending can connect you to a story of hope and dignity. Visit their site to learn more.

● **End the blame game.** Visit www .tenshekelshirt.com to view the video of the song "Fragile" by the band 10 Shekel Shirt. Consider your current understanding of issues around trafficking, drug addiction, and racism as you view the video.

LIVE

● **Act on what you've learned.** Join the social justice committee at your place of worship. If there isn't one, consider partnering with an adult to start one. Check with missions coordinators for insight about how to establish a local outreach program in your community of faith.

● **Read ... and then act.** Select a book from the list on page 43 of this guide and host a book club to learn how other people have put their compassion into action to combat injustices around the globe.

● **Go glocal.** Turn your group into a "glocal" community by thinking globally and acting locally. Agree to meet once a month to discuss one pressing global issue, such as the ones in this study. During your meetings, pray over the people groups being affected, and then commit to taking action to help alleviate an evident problem they face. Better still, have a culturally relevant meal with each group meeting!

LEAD

● **Rally your block.** Organize a get together such as a block party with your friends and neighbors and invite a local outreach coordinator to be the speaker. Ask him or her to explain opportunities that exist in your own backyard for fighting for others' basic human rights.

● **Host a justice meal.** Have your church or ministry team host a simple meal (visit www.worldvision.org and search "Broken Bread" for ideas) and ask the participants to make a donation that will be given to a local organization that works for justice in your community.

● **Leverage other people's work.** Host a panel discussion with several leaders who are already putting their compassion into action in the fight against human trafficking.

start> Ready for More?

> Read

- *Just Courage*, Gary Haugen
- *Not for Sale*, David Batstone
- *Be the Change*, Zach Hunter
- *Washed by Blood*, Brian "Head" Welch
- *A Heart Set Free*, David Leyden

> Watch

- *The Blind Side* (PG-13)
- *End of the Spear* (PG-13)
- *The Mission* (PG)
- *We Were Free* (International Justice Mission, NR)

> Surf

- www.startproject.org
- www.ijm.org
- www.notforsalecampaign.org
- www.freetheslaves.net
- www.zachhunter.me

4

Honoring the Poor

> "We may forget that the poor are not an abstraction but rather a group of human beings who have names, who are made in the image of God, whose hairs are numbered, and for whom Jesus died."
>
> — Bryant Myers, author of *Walking with the Poor*

 Group Time

 Get Connected   1 minute

Have someone in the group read aloud this brief description of the session theme.

There are approximately seven billion people in the world today, and more than three billion of them — close to half — live on less than two dollars a day. It's an overwhelming statistic, reflecting an overwhelming problem — namely, that too many people are forced to survive on too few resources. "The poor will *always* be with us," overwhelmed people say. "The best efforts will *still* be in vain." It's an understandable way to think, but it comes at a terribly high cost.

Jesus' idea when he sent out his followers — and you — to reach the world with his message of grace was that they would *put off* their selfish concerns and sinful desires and *put on* compassion for a broken and needy world. Following him means following the example that he set — feeding hungry people, clothing people who crave warmth, and providing resources to people who are poor.

You've likely been entrusted with much. And a needy world is waiting to see if you will be Christ to them. Poverty is real and its devastating effects are seen on all sides.

Your actions matter. Your choices matter. Choose today to **start>**.

> Know Your Neighbor   2 minutes

Using one or two words, answer the following question about the session theme.

What do the poor have to offer the rest of society?

> *"Speak up for those who cannot speak for themselves, for the rights of all who are destitute. Speak up and judge fairly; defend the rights of the poor and needy."*
>
> —Proverbs 31:8 – 9

> Give Your Heart and Mind to God   1 minute

Addressing the needs of those trapped in cyclical poverty first must begin with genuine submission to the King of compassion, Jesus Christ. Ask God to tenderize your heart to the stories, the facts, and the realities that will be presented in this session's DVD segment. And then request wisdom for knowing how to respond — personally, genuinely, and with great passion for those who are poor.

 **Learn Together** 20 minutes

If you'd like to take notes as you watch the session 4 video segment, use the space below.

> Discuss "Honoring the Poor"　　　　30 minutes

1. According to the video segment, Steve Chalke realized from the moment he surrendered his life to Jesus that the gospel is good news — socially and emotionally and physically, as *well* as spiritually. Based on your unique personality, predispositions, and life experiences, which of those four areas of faith does your life tend to reflect? Select from the following list any that apply:

❏ **Social** > "I practice and encourage moral, ethical, and good behavior."

❏ **Emotional** > "Through words and sometimes deeds, I encourage peace of mind and heart."

❏ **Physical** > "I invest significant time and energy providing help to people in need."

❏ **Spiritual** > "I pray for people living far from God, for their salvation and for the living out of their life's purpose."

As you consider the area(s) of faith you selected, think about what assumptions or experiences play into how faith most often is seen in your life. For example, perhaps the church you grew up in placed great emphasis on prayer but never engaged in showing practical compassion to people in need in your community. As a result, from an early age your faith seemed to bend more toward spiritual reflection than physical action. Jot down your thoughts below, and then share with the group an example or two that came to mind.

2. As it relates to easing the burden of people living in poverty, Steve Chalke said that we grow only as we serve others. How have you found this to be true or untrue in your life?

3. If *serving God by serving others* indeed is a goal for followers of Jesus, then what attitudes or actions do you believe help move a person toward a lifestyle of service?

> Now Is the Time   5 minutes

This is the most important part of the session — deciding how you and your group will choose to live like the Good Samaritan.

In the video segment Jarrett Stevens said, "When you and I begin to see the poor and under resourced and overlooked not as a problem, not as a project, but as a people, then we begin to see the face of Jesus in them." Furthermore, when we do this, "we will see Jesus like we never have seen him before. In ways that will change the way we see ourselves."

These words issue a clear challenge to Jesus followers, and they cause us to ask ourselves difficult questions.

Do you want to see Jesus like you have never seen him before?

Do you want to see Jesus in ways that will change the way you see yourself?

How will you respond?

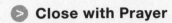 **Close with Prayer**   1 minute

The end of your time together is now the beginning of incredible Good Samaritan possibilities for you and your group. Take a moment to say a prayer to God, saying thank you for what you have learned and committing your life to living like the Good Samaritan.

*Living out your faith in real and tangible ways is more than just doing a DVD study — it is a lifelong journey. The "Personal Time" section is your guide as you go forward on this quest. Of course, like any journey, this one will be easier and more fruitful with the support and encouragement of others. **startproject.org** is that community. There you'll find other stories and testimonies just like yours, links to organizations and people who need your help and special skills, and opportunities to Learn, Live, and Lead a Good Samaritan life.*

To reconnect with this session's topic as you dive into the "start> Now" section, answer the questions below.

1. Mike Yankoski said that one of the most meaningful deeds a stranger could do for people who are poor is simply to notice them, to treat them as human beings. Have you ever considered the simple act of "noticing someone" to be a good deed? When have you felt "noticed" by a stranger, and how did the eye contact or words or actions make you feel? Record your responses in the space below.

2. Shane Claiborne encouraged followers of Jesus to find their "Calcutta," whether that looks like a slum in India or a home for elderly people down the street from where you live. Based on

what you've experienced in this curriculum so far, how would you describe the "Calcutta" where God might be calling you to serve?

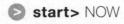 **start>** NOW

*Everyone must **start>** at the beginning, which means going from little or no knowledge to enough understanding to be able to make wise decisions. In each session, this portion of the Personal Time will provide you with resources and links to a wealth of important information.*

LEARN

● **Explore homelessness.** Read the book *Under the Overpass*, by Mike Yankoski. What thoughts and convictions swirl in your mind and heart as you read his words? Where does Jesus' claim in Matthew 5:3 ("blessed are the poor in spirit") intersect the themes of Mike's writing?

● **Write God's Word on your heart.** Memorize a portion of verses in Acts 2–4.

Among the early church communities, no one was in need. Who is in need in your family or on your block? What resources could you share with them today?

● **Join forces with your church.** Check with your church to find out what God is already doing to serve those with tremendous needs in your community. How might God be prompting you to join forces in alleviating suffering?

LIVE

● **Leverage a line.** While you are waiting in a line at school or at a coffee shop, strike up a conversation with the person next to you simply to find a way to encourage him or her in the moment.

● **Scour your street.** Take a friend or parent and interview the five people who live closest to your home in order to uncover as many needs as possible. Who is a single mom? Who just lost his job? Who needs help caring for disabled children? Ask God to guide you toward meeting one of those needs.

● **Care for a child.** Sponsor a child through an organization such as World Vision (www.worldvision.org). Make an individual commitment, or consider sponsoring one or two children along with your friends or family.

LEAD

● **Try friend raising!** Rather than raising funds, try your hand at "friend raising." Share your passion for serving the poor with people in your sphere of influence and challenge them to serve alongside you this week.

● **Be a voice for the homeless.** Invite your friends to join you in writing a letter to your city council, mayor, or congressperson addressing an area of concern for under resourced people in your community.

● **Host a 30-Hour Famine.** Bring World Vision's 30-Hour Famine to your church and grow closer to Christ while engaging in an international movement to fight hunger. You'll fast for thirty hours while raising funds to feed and care for children around the world. To sign up, visit www.30hourfamine.org.

start> Ready for More?

> Read

- *Under the Overpass*, Mike Yankoski
- *Starving Jesus*, Craig Gross
- *Make Poverty Personal*, Ash Barker
- *A Chance to Die*, Elisabeth Elliot
- *Tell Them Who I Am*, Elliot Liebow

> Watch

- *The Soloist* (PG-13)
- *The Pursuit of Happyness* (PG-13)
- *Where God Left His Shoes* (NR)
- *Faith Like Potatoes* (PG)
- *The Grapes of Wrath* (NR)

> Surf

- www.startproject.org
- www.worldvision.org
- www.bread.org
- www.one.org
- www.wordmadeflesh.org

5

Caring for
God's Creation

> "I often hear people tell me that they don't think that their individual efforts can make a difference....But the truth is that every action makes a difference. We just need to start."
>
> —Thomas Kostigen, author of *You Are Here: Exposing the Vital Link Between What We Do and What That Does to Our Planet*

 start> Group Time

 Get Connected   1 minute

Have someone in the group read aloud this brief description of the session theme.

In Genesis 2:15, God placed a man in the Garden of Eden to "work it and take care of it." Despite the clarity of that phrase, many followers of Jesus today live as though they exist on a planet that can be wasted and behave as though they will never be held accountable for how they care for God's creation.

But hope is still alive. As you dive into the subject of creation care, open your heart and your mind to the ways in which we as Christians who love and serve Christ can shape our personal lives in creation-friendly ways by conserving resources and practicing creation-friendly habits. And be encouraged as you experience afresh the joy of connecting with the natural world God himself formed.

Your actions matter. Your choices matter. Choose today to **start>**.

> Know Your Neighbor   2 minutes

Using one or two words, answer the following question about the session theme.

What one word comes to mind when you hear the term "environmentalist?"

"The earth is the LORD's, and everything in it."

—Psalm 24:1

> Give Your Heart and Mind to God   1 minute

Creation care can be a tricky topic to discuss with followers of Jesus because for many people, the issue seems political and controversial. As you begin your group time, resubmit your mind and heart to the authority of God. Invite him to move and stir as his Spirit pleases. Ask him to remove all distractions — noises, homework, issues with your parents, tomorrow's concerns, as well as preconceived ideas about the topic of creation care — and to calm your soul as you experience session 5.

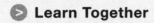

Becoming a Good Samaritan

> Learn Together   20 minutes

If you'd like to take notes as you watch the session 5 video segment, use the space below.

> Discuss "Caring for God's Creation"   30 minutes

1. Think back on the assumptions aired by your group at the beginning of this session. How were they validated or challenged by the DVD content? Note your response in the space below before sharing it with your group.

2. During the video segment, session teacher Matthew Sleeth made the comment, "There are now no elms on Elm Street, no chestnuts on Chestnut Street, and no caribou left in Caribou, Maine." In your own surroundings, how do you see evidence of environmental change?

3. Read the words of Psalm 65:8 – 13 below and then answer the questions that follow.

    The whole earth is filled with awe at your wonders; where morning dawns, where evening fades, you call forth songs of joy. You care for the land and water it; you enrich it abundantly. The streams of God are filled with water to provide the people with grain, for so you have ordained it. You drench its furrows and level its ridges; you soften it with showers and bless its crops. You crown the year with your bounty, and your carts overflow with abundance. The grasslands of the wilderness overflow; the hills are clothed with gladness. The meadows are covered with flocks and the valleys are mantled with grain; they shout for joy and sing.

    What do you believe is the role of a follower of Jesus in ensuring that "grasslands overflow" and that "hills are clothed with gladness" in this generation and generations to come? Write down your thoughts in the space below before sharing them with your group.

How does the "dominion" that humankind was given in the Genesis account relate to life today? In other words, what does having "dominion...over all the earth" and all of the creatures in it (Genesis 1:26 King James Version) mean practically for a teen graduating from high school or for you specifically? Discuss your thoughts with your group, jotting down themes that surface in the space below.

 ## Now Is the Time

5 minutes

This is the most important part of the session — deciding how you and your group will choose to live like the Good Samaritan.

We've come to rely on (and love) technology. Take a few minutes to brainstorm as a group all of the appliances and electronic gadgets that did not exist five or ten years ago that you "couldn't live without" today. Then select one appliance or piece of electronic equipment and suspend use of it from now until when your group meets again.

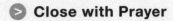

> **Close with Prayer** 1 minute

The end of your time together is now the beginning of incredible Good Samaritan possibilities for you and your group. Take a moment to say a prayer to God, saying thank you for what you have learned and committing your life to living like the Good Samaritan.

start> Personal Time

Living out your faith in real and tangible ways is more than just doing a DVD study—it is a lifelong journey. The "Personal Time" section is your guide as you go forward on this quest. Of course, like any journey, this one will be easier and more fruitful with the support and encouragement of others. **startproject.org** *is that community. There you'll find other stories and testimonies just like yours, links to organizations and people who need your help and special skills, and opportunities to Learn, Live, and Lead a Good Samaritan life.*

To reconnect with this session's topic as you dive into the "start> Now" section, answer the following questions.

1. Emergency-room-doctor-turned-environmentalist Matthew Sleeth mentioned that he's rarely heard the terms "tree hugger" and "Christian" used lovingly in the same sentence. Why do you suppose this is? Record your thoughts in the space below.

2. Shirley Mullen, president of Houghton College, said that "creation care requires faithfulness to new habits, and faithfulness is not something that any of us is very good at by ourselves." In the space below, jot down the names of two or three people who might be willing to explore a few new creation care habits. Choose one of them to tell about your "appliance ban."

> start> NOW

*Everyone must **start>** at the beginning, which means going from little or no knowledge to enough understanding to be able to make wise decisions. In each session, this portion of the Personal Time will provide you with resources and links to a wealth of important information.*

LEARN

● **Consider yourself a steward.** Make a list of your favorite "possessions" and record your ideas about how they might be used to impact the kingdom. How might your life look different if you truly believed that every resource you "possess" is really a gift from God to be stewarded well? Journal your thoughts.

● **See what Scripture says.** Visit www.creationcare.org to find out what the Bible says about stewarding planet Earth. Jot down a meaningful verse on a card that you keep on the fridge, your bathroom mirror, or somewhere prominent in your room.

● **Have a candid conversation.** Discuss with a friend or family member how your resources might be impacting your world positively and which ones might be having a negative effect. Consider resources such as your finances, time, car, house, trash, energy use, and so forth.

LIVE

● **Unplug!** Unplug all electronics and power strips when they are not in use to avoid incurring electricity costs for what is called the "phantom load."

● **Recycle!** Grab a box or bin, put it in an out-of-the-way corner, and begin training yourself to think before you discard something in the trash.

● **Compost it!** Instead of shoving food scraps down the food disposer this week, talk to your parents about trying your hand at composting. Then, use the by-products of your work in a plant or vegetable garden. Visit www .howtocompost.org for information on how to get going.

LEAD

● **Share and share alike.** Try sharing resources with friends and family. How would sharing items impact your relationships and the world around you?

● **Go clean, go green.** Organize a "Clean and Green" day with friends, your family, your neighbors, and others. Devote a day to cleaning up a church campus, a street, a neighborhood, or a public park. Organize **start>** groups in your neighborhood! Be the spark that sets your sphere of influence ablaze for issues of creation care.

● **Request recycling.** Write letters to your city officials requesting recycling services in your neighborhood.

start> Ready for More?

> Read

- *It's Easy Being Green*, Emma Sleeth
- *The Gospel According to the Earth*, Matthew Sleeth
- *Green Like God*, Jonathan Merritt
- *For the Beauty of the Earth*, Steven Bouma-Prediger
- *Saving God's Green Earth*, Tri Robinson

> Watch

- *Oceans* (G)
- *Earth* (G)
- *March of the Penguins* (G)
- *WALL-E* (G)
- *Planet Earth* (NR)

> Surf

- www.startproject.org
- www.blessedearth.org
- www.flourishonline.org
- www.earthministry.org
- www.arocha.org

6

Loving the forsaken

> "The times we find ourselves having to wait on others may be the perfect opportunities to train ourselves to wait on the Lord."
>
> — Joni Eareckson Tada, founder, Joni & Friends ministry

 start *Group Time*

> **Get Connected** 1 minute

Have someone in the group read aloud this brief description of the session theme.

Amid busy lives that yield jam-packed days, it is easy to focus only on your own tasks, troubles, needs, and plans. Session 6 invites you to look at the world from a vastly different vantage point — through the eyes of "unloved others."

God calls his people to represent Jesus Christ not just to people who look the same, act the same, and talk the same, but to *every* man, *every* woman, and *every* child who needs his care.

Your actions matter. Your choices matter. Choose today to **start>**.

> **Know Your Neighbor** 2 minutes

Using one or two words, answer the following question about the session theme.

What does it mean to be "disenfranchised"?

"Religion that God our Father accepts as pure and faultless is this: to look after orphans and widows in their distress and to keep oneself from being polluted by the world."

— James 1:27

> **Give Your Heart and Mind to God** 1 minute

It sometimes seems easier to consider those who are widowed, orphaned, and incarcerated as "categories" instead of as the crown of all creation, but those who love God are called to adopt an altogether different mind-set. As you prepare to work through session 6, ask him for eyes that are open so that you see suffering people as God sees them, for ears that hear clearly the stories that break God's heart, and for arms that will stretch themselves toward embracing people as Jesus Christ did when he walked upon the earth. At some point every follower of Jesus was in need of adoption, tenderness, and release from bondage. Remember how you felt then and let God use that empathy for good during this session.

 **Learn Together**   20 minutes

If you'd like to take notes as you watch the session 6 video segment, use the space below.

> **Discuss "Loving the Forsaken"**   30 minutes

1. Session teacher Jim Cymbala said that the "only advertisement for Christ on this earth is we Christians — the body of Christ, the church of the Lord." What do you want that "billboard" to communicate to the watching world? Note your answer below and then share what you wrote with your group.

2. Now write a message that reflects what you think the *watching world* sees when they "read" Christians' lives.

3. As it relates to those who are disenfranchised among you, why do you suppose there is a difference between what Christians *wish* their billboards said and what the watching world *actually* sees? Discuss your thoughts with the entire group, noting below the ideas you hear that resonate with you the most.

4. In the video segment, Jim Cymbala said, "The greatest expression of love is to reach out to those who are soiled and unworthy and to lift them up with love." Think about a time when God himself reached out to you along the way and lifted you up with love. Describe the experience in the space below before sharing it with your group.

5. What is your most recent memory of another *person* "lifting you up" with love?

> Now Is the Time   5 minutes

This is the most important part of the session — deciding how you and your group will choose to live like the Good Samaritan.

In the video segment Jeanne Stevens said, "When you see that you have something to give … you start to become a part of the solution instead of the problem."

As you finish this session and close this study, it is time to think and pray about how you will move forward. As you do so, it is important to remember the following questions:

1. *Who is a neighbor?*
2. *What does a neighbor do?*

These are the questions at the heart of the parable of the Good Samaritan, and the answers Jesus gives are clear and challenging:

Everyone can be a neighbor.

A neighbor is one who shows mercy to people in need.

Choose today to live like the Good Samaritan!

Your actions matter. Your choices matter. Choose today to **start>**.

Close with Prayer   1 minute

The end of your time together is now the beginning of incredible Good Samaritan possibilities for you and your group. Take a moment to say a prayer to God, saying thank you for what you have learned and committing your life to living like the Good Samaritan.

Living out your faith in real and tangible ways is more than just doing a DVD study — it is a lifelong journey. The "Personal Time" section is your guide as you go forward on this quest. Of course, like any journey, this one will be easier and more fruitful with the support and encouragement of others. **startproject.org** *is that community. There you'll find other stories and testimonies just like yours, links to organizations and people who need your help and special skills, and opportunities to Learn, Live, and Lead a Good Samaritan life.*

To reconnect with this session's topic as you dive into the "start> Now" section, answer the following questions.

1. Jim Cymbala said that when he thinks of all the love that God has shown him, despite his many fumblings and failings, it becomes even more important to show love to others. What attitudes or actions are stirred in you when you consider the love that God has shown you?

2. Chuck Colson said, "It is a blessing to give of ourselves, and to see how God uses us to bless other people in our lives." When was the last time you experienced the blessing of blessing another person's life? How might God want to use that experience as motivation for you to continue being a blessing in others' lives?

> start> NOW

*Everyone must **start>** at the beginning, which means going from little or no knowledge to enough understanding to be able to make wise decisions. In each session, this portion of the Personal Time will provide you with resources and links to a wealth of important information.*

LEARN

● **Gather up hope.** Watch stories of transformation from around the globe, produced by Prison Fellowship International (www.theprisonyard.org).

● **Take note of paths you've crossed.** For one day, make a list of every person with whom you cross paths, including the friend you met for lunch as well as the people on the street who pass by. Whether you know their names or not, whether you engaged them in conversation or not, write down what you saw about their situations, as well as what you imagine God saw.

● **Read of ragamuffins.** Read Brennan Manning's *The Ragamuffin Gospel.* Note your thoughts on what it means to love others as God loves them in a journal as you read.

LIVE

● **Turn gossip into action.** What you chatter about might just reveal how you could get involved. Next time you find yourself sermonizing to others, stop and ask God, "Is this a place I am supposed to serve or a problem I should try to solve?"

● **Look like Luke 16:10.** God desires that you use your resources to advance *his* kingdom rather than your own. Commit a portion of your funds to someone in need this week.

● **Deliver meals on wheels.** Those who are homebound or hospitalized love to see a friendly smile. Browse www.mowaa.org and, if possible, consider helping at a local Meals on Wheels program this week.

LEAD

● **Become a pen pal.** Form a team of pen pals within your small group or larger faith community. Choose a group of people who might need an extra dose of hope and encouragement; for example, you could sponsor a child through World Vision. Then write to him or her on a monthly basis.

● **Book worms, unite!** Start a book club that dives into books such as *Hunger for Healing, Trolls and Truth*, or *Same Kind of Different as Me* to continue to cultivate understanding of your own brokenness and a deeper level of compassion toward others.

● **Let your experience shine.** Organize a tutoring group/ministry that will assist children. Volunteer to stay after school and help with after-school programs.

start> Ready for More?

> Read

- *You Were Made for More*, Jim Cymbala
- *The Me I Want to Be, Teen Edition*, John Ortberg
- *Take Your Best Shot*, Austin Gutwein
- *The Search for Significance: Student Edition*, Robert S. McGee
- *The Saddest Girl in the World*, Cathy Glass

> Watch

- *Radio* (PG)
- *I Am Sam* (PG-13)
- *Temple Grandin* (TV-PG)
- *Lean on Me* (PG-13)
- *Simon Birch* (PG)

> Surf

- www.startproject.org
- www.prisonyard.org
- www.pfi.org
- www.joniandfriends.org
- www.angeltree.org

Journal

Journal

Journal

Journal

Journal

Journal

Journal

Journal

Journal

Journal

Journal

Journal

Journal

Journal

Journal

Share Your Thoughts

With the Author: Your comments will be forwarded to the author when you send them to *zauthor@zondervan.com*.

With Zondervan: Submit your review of this book by writing to *zreview@zondervan.com*.

Free Online Resources at
www.zondervan.com

Zondervan AuthorTracker: Be notified whenever your favorite authors publish new books, go on tour, or post an update about what's happening in their lives.

Daily Bible Verses and Devotions: Enrich your life with daily Bible verses or devotions that help you start every morning focused on God.

Free Email Publications: Sign up for newsletters on fiction, Christian living, church ministry, parenting, and more.

Zondervan Bible Search: Find and compare Bible passages in a variety of translations at www.zondervanbiblesearch.com.

Other Benefits: Register yourself to receive online benefits like coupons and special offers, or to participate in research.